Hoodoo For Beginners

Learn the Secrets to Magic Spells in Rootwork and Conjure With Roots, Herbs, Candles, and Oils

Brian Loza

advice, counsel, strategies and techniques that may be offered in this volume.

TABLE OF CONTENTS

INTRODUCTION

During the 17th and 18th centuries, many people were trafficked out of Africa and forced into slavery. They were forced to leave behind their land, their families, their friends, and everything that they knew to work as servants in a new world with new people that they barely understood. Much of their culture was quashed as a result. Stability was little more than a dream for these people in a strange land. They were forced to comply with what the slave owners demanded. They were forced to forsake their own culture.

With as many different people from as many different lands all brought together as if they were the same, forced to comply, and being endangered constantly, it is no surprise that they brought together what they would. These slaves came together, developing their own cultural ways of attempting to take control of a situation that seemed utterly uncontrollable. They created what is known as hoodoo.

Hoodoo was created to provide protection. It was meant to heal. Though commonly referred to or depicted as evil, the truth is, this slander was little more than the attempt to get the world to believe that all culture from the Africans was bad. It was an attempt to subvert and eliminate any identity that the African slaves had. However, the truth is that the slaves often turned to Hoodoo as their attempt to maintain some semblance of control in a world where they were unable to control anything at all.

Hoodoo, also known as rootwork, is a form of ancestral alchemy. It incorporates a combination of divination, mediumship, and herbalism to create the effects of protection and healing. It is used primarily for love, protection, healing, and money, and though it is possible to direct the powers toward others in ways that are meant to protect you by returning negative energy to those who cast it in the first place.

As you read through this book, you will be welcomed to the world of hoodoo. Now, it is something that is not accessible to all—if you want to be able to practice rootwork, you have to first have your own ancestral ties to it. It is that ancestral tie that makes it as powerful as it is, and if you do not have that connection, you cannot truly tap into the power known as rootwork.

You will be brought into understanding what Hoodoo is, what the tools are, and how to begin practicing. We will be going over the importance of herbs and how they are used, as well as how you can begin to create your very own rootwork. Rootworkers are powerful, and the connection to the ancestors is incredibly appealing to many with those roots in the first place.

This book will give you the power that you are looking for, and you will be able to tap into it. You will have that connection that you are looking for. Are you ready to connect back to your ancestors? Are you ready to bring some peace into your life? This is how you make it happen.

Thank you for taking the time to read through this book, and hopefully, you will find the answers that you are looking for.

CHAPTER 1: WHAT IS HOODOO?

Rootwork. Conjure. Hoodoo.

These are all words for the same thing, and it can be used in fantastic and mysterious ways. If you are one of those who had descended from the African slaves brought to the United States when slavery was legal, then you have the ancestral ties that can connect you to hoodoo. Those people, desperate to maintain some degree of their various cultures, worked together. In the strange, new land, they did not know what the plants were, how they worked, or what the various talismans or curios they could make were. The slaves learned more during their time together and discovered plenty about the uses of the various herbs that are native to the United States.

They used what they found, and as you study hoodoo, you will see that the majority of the plants, curios, and other added factors are primarily based upon what you would find available in the Deep South, where slavery was the most prevalent. In their need for protection, for cures, and for their own sense of control over the world, they focused on understanding the world around them and focused on building up their own practices to allow them to gain that sort of answer to their perceived powerlessness.

Understanding Hoodoo requires you to first understand the history it brought with it. It requires you to understand the most prevalent influences that come into play so you will be able to recognize what it is. And, in learning to understand the roots behind it, you can start practicing yourself. We will be addressing the most common and most fundamental concepts here in this chapter. From the history of Hoodoo to understanding who the rootworkers were and who they are today, and more, you will discover the most fundamental information that is going to prepare you for your entrance into the world of hoodoo.

A History of Hoodoo

The origins of Hoodoo begins with the estimated 388,000 African people, from all sorts of different ethnic groups, who were shipped from Africa to North America between the 17th and 19th centuries. Thanks to the transatlantic slave trade, people from various cultures were all bunched together. Between the cultures from the Indigenous Americans and the enslaved Africans, many different belief systems came together.

As these cultures came together, they began sharing their beliefs. Especially in regions where the enslaved Africans were relatively isolated, they were allowed to retain more of their West African beliefs. This was common in the Southeast in particular, and especially in the Mississippi Delta; the high concentration of slavery allowed for the enslaved to come together in secrecy more often.

The more they interacted together, the more they were able to bring together various aspects of their cultures, and by 1875, the word "hoodoo" had entered American English to refer to this sort of manifestation of power. Especially in African-American Vernacular English, it was found to refer to that sort of paranormal element or spiritual spells.

There is a rich culture behind hoodoo, and it all begins with origins in Africa. In particular, the Dahomean people from Western Africa once engaged in both medicinal and religious practices that are related to hoodoo. From the core beliefs to the implementation of rituals and the utilization of plants and curios, there are many parallels between the two, which becomes even more prevalent when considering the discussion of ancestors.

Dahomean legends also included information about deities and intermediaries that remained prevalent in Hoodoo as well. In particular, one such deity was Legba, who also maintained relevancy in both New Orleans Voodoo and Haitian Vodou as a sort of intermediary between both the physical and spiritual realms. This very same deity exists in Hoodoo as well—the Black Man at the Crossroads shares that very same function and legends, though the name has been removed.

Vodou and other such African religions were quickly crushed by the slave owners who were trying to retain control over their slaves. Threatened by any sort of foreign religion, the slaves were forced to convert to Christianity. However, that was not enough for them to stop practicing the rootwork they were developing themselves.

Hoodoo lives on today—it is passed down from generation to generation, and it is that very interaction between generations that works to give it the power. The rootworkers are able to influence the results of reality. Through ancestral practices, the rootworkers gain that influence over how the events in the world play out. In particular, Hoodoo is actually on the rise as the Black community continues to reclaim their own culture from appropriation. Thanks to writers such as Zora Neale Hurston, the effort to preserve Hoodoo practice has allowed for the revival. And, thanks to the prevalence of the internet now, it is much more possible than it was before to maintain those connections, discover the practices, and find others interested in practicing or who already do.

Hoodoo vs. Voodoo

Now, before we continue, it is essential that we stop and consider the fact that Hoodoo and voodoo are entirely different concepts and practices altogether. Though they are commonly assumed to be the same thing, voodoo, sometimes spelled as Vodou, voudun, and voudou, is an entirely separate practice that is actually a religion. It originates in Haiti but has its own West African ties.

Voodoo itself has several specific practices that require ordainment to perform. There are also religious leaders that will oversee these practices, just as there are leaders overseeing other religions. There are also spirits and deities that get their own worshipping in voodoo. The leaders, known as mambos and houngans, are there to guide the followers to give voodoo that specific structure.

Hoodoo, though similar, is not a religion. It is several practices instead that, though it has spiritual influence and is spiritual in nature. There is a belief in spirits present in hoodoo and the belief that life is created via energy. This energy is important to the practice of Hoodoo as well. However, despite that, there is no organization. You do not have certain worships that you have to do. You do not have to worship specific gods—any gods can be followed, and as you will see, this is how rootworkers were able to practice, even while eventually converting to Christianity, and you will see this influence.

Hoodoo and Christianity

Most slave owners were Christian. In an attempt to maintain further control, many forced their slaves to follow the same practices. In fact, several slaves found themselves forbidden from practicing their own religions under the threat of being killed if they were caught. They were forced to comply with the religion of those around them. They had to work hard to disguise their actions within the confines of Christianity. In order to follow their beliefs, they needed to make them compatible with the Protestants around them. This worked in many different ways.

In particular, there is the prevalence of God and His providence present in hoodoo. Some Hoodoo practitioners even use Psalms as a way to focus their magic. Conjure represented a way that the rootworkers could comply with the need to convert, and in some cases, comply with the religions that they had accepted relatively easily, while still maintaining those roots back to their traditional beliefs. Conjure allowed the enslaved to maintain a degree of control. It was a symbolic means to address their own suffering that they had to endure. It allowed for defense from harm and was able to help them maintain power.

Many Hoodoo practitioners that you will meet today do have religious ties to Christianity. They believe that Christian and Catholic saints are just more spirits that exist in the world and that the Bible is another powerful book. They may go to church regularly and practice their Christianity readily—and there are no contradictions to doing so with their practicing of conjure.

Who are the Rootworkers?

Hoodoo practitioners are the hoodoos or the rootworkers. They practice Hoodoo and use spells, known as roots. The strength of their roots is what gives them their power. The energy and power of Hoodoo are in the mojo, and it runs through families. Those who have stronger mojo are able to pass it down better than those who may not. This means that more isolated communities, such as the Gullahs of South Carolina, are much more able to pass on the traditions rooted in conjure.

It is that tie to the ancestors and spirits that create a sort of shield of protection, passed down primarily by women, though not restricted by gender. However, in the past, it was persecuted as "witchcraft" and corrupted. The white men were quick to paint Hoodoo as "black magic" and "evil," but the truth is, it is only black in the sense that the practitioners have black skin.

Hoodoo Beliefs

Though Hoodoo itself is not a religion, there are connections to religions that can be understood as well. Some of the primary beliefs that allow for the cultivation of the magic and power of Hoodoo include those listed here.

Divine providence

Most rootworkers believe that there is some sort of higher power, which may be the Christian God or could be some other as well. Remember, there are no required deities that must be followed in order to practice hoodoo. Some believe that the deities and spirits from all religions are available to draw from. The deities are believed to be interested in human lives and have the power to alter the course of action as well, and that means that they are actively going to be involved. Because of this involvement, they may be petitioned as well.

Life after death

There is also a belief that the soul continues to exist after the death of the body. This is essential to the understanding of ancestral spirits that can be called upon. Most rootworkers begin with learning to work with the spirits through first working with their direct ancestors. In hoodoo, it is believed that rather than dying completely, there is a degree of ascendance instead; the ancestors may have passed physically, but they are still present in our lives, guiding their newest generation carefully and may also be able to protect us as well when necessary.

Divination

Divination is the ability to understand what will, or what is likely to, happen in the future. It is the utilization of communication with the spirits to begin understanding how the events are playing out to allow for that prediction to occur. It is one of the most powerful parts of Hoodoo magic, as once you know what is likely to happen, you can start influencing what is happening to better achieve whatever it is that you have set out to attain in your own attempts to practice. If you want to ensure that your desired end is achieved, you have to be able to influence the odds to make it so, and that is what this power is for.

Doctrine of signatures

The doctrine of signatures is the belief that everything has a signature. That is to say, every single thing in existence in the world around us has been marked by the Creator, whether that Creator is the universe, a God, or something else. The mark will allow its use to be observed and implied just by virtue of knowing what the shape is. Anything, from seeing the shape of the roots to recognize where it grows or what it is called, can be used to begin ascertaining the true purpose and use of that particular item. This is especially prevalent when considering plants or the utilization of curios, allowing for that understanding to influence their uses in rootwork.

Retributive justice

Retributive justice is the idea that if something happens to you, there is an equal punishment. Think of the Biblical principle of an eye for an eye—it is that idea that when someone wrongs you, then they ought to be wronged in the same fashion. While other forms of religion and magic require adherence to the idea of not harming

others, in hoodoo, it is entirely acceptable, and even expected, for those to protect themselves through magic, and they are allowed to retaliate against those who first harmed them. However, if you are retaliating, it must be of equal level.

Intention

When using hoodoo, the idea of curses is a wish that may only be fulfilled by God when deserved. You may lay down powders to cause a curse, but they will only work on those who they were intended to work on. Even if others walk on those powders, if they were not the intended recipient, or if they were undeserving, they will not be effective. This is related to Proverbs 26:2, which states:

"Like a fluttering sparrow or a darting swallow, an undeserved curse does not come to rest."

What this means is that if you try to curse someone who is undeserving, relating right back to the principle of retributive justice, it will not work. If the curse does not work, you can then presume that the curse was not deserved.

Who Can Practice Hoodoo?

Remember this—rootwork is not a religion. It is a practice that is inherited solely by birth line. You are born into being able to practice hoodoo. You are born into a line of family members that likely has some sort of history with hoodoo. In particular, if you have no descendants of Africans enslaved in the United States, you lack the spiritual connection that you would need. Without that spiritual connection, how can you call upon your ancestors? Though some recipes may claim that they have a European influence, remember that the Europeans segregated the enslaved Africans—they were kept entirely separate and therefore did not socialize. Those recipes that claim that they have European influence are a dead giveaway that they are not actually authentic Hoodoo recipes.

CHAPTER 2: THE BASIC SUPPLIES

When you are ready to practice hoodoo, you must first begin gathering the tools and supplies that you are likely to require during your practices. Not all spells will require all of these supplies, but this chapter will go over the bulk of those that you will need. Remember, everything in this world has some sort of divine signature—they all have purposes, and when you learn to recognize the purposes, you will start drawing from their powers.

Keep in mind that when you are purchasing supplies that you are likely to use, you may or may not have luck in person. If you do not live somewhere that has a prevalent community rooted in hoodoo, you might struggle to find what you are looking for locally. However, thankfully, you also have access to the entirety of the internet in the palms of your hands. Do not be afraid to look online for the products that you will need if you cannot find them locally, but also be mindful that what you are buying is authentic.

Now, let's take a look at the basics. From oils to candles and everything in between, the various options for tools that you have got to ensure that you communicate with the spirits and start to see the results that you are looking for are here for you. You just have to know where to look and what to get.

Conjure Oils

Oils are not unique to Hoodoo and are actually prevalent in most religions for various purposes. In hoodoo, they are typically used as either an accelerant or as a sealant. This means that when you put certain oils on certain people, places, or things, you then accelerate or increase the power of the rootwork that you are trying to perform. You can also use it as a method of sealing the power that you have just directed as well. This is the consecration process and will allow you to maintain the power in items to ensure that you can use them later.

There are various types of oils for all sorts of purposes. They are extracted from certain plants, and as such, they have their own unique properties and powers. Remember that everything has a purpose, whether it is invoking certain emotions or creating certain settings. They are typically used to anoint or dress. When you dress something, you simply place the oil onto it while also working the necessary ritual. We will see more of this toward the end of the book as we begin to discuss the spells that you can create.

However, oils are not always the most suitable medium to use. You cannot exactly put oil onto paper and assume that you will have it work, after all. Some Hoodoo rootwork is meant to aid in the business realm, and if you tried anointing your bills or invoices or receipts with oil, they would appear to be soiled and may actually cause you more problems. In that instance, the powder may be the better option.

When you are working with candle magic, on the other hand, using oil is an option that you have. You can use the oil to sprinkle onto the candle, allowing the burning of the candle to activate. They can also be used in mojo bags to help their power as well.

If you wished to create your own oils, you could do this as well. However, you will need some sort of neutral base. A commonly used one is coconut oil, which is quite adaptable based upon what is added to it. It is incredibly versatile and can be used for anything from gentle love potions to more powerful options. As you will see later in this book, there are many different options that you can use for all sorts of purposes. To create your oils, you would simply use a transparent glass bottle and then add in your oil, followed by all of the herbs or plants that you intended to use. Then, allow them to sit in the bottle overnight. You would then strain the whole mixture into a new container, keeping the plant matter out, repeating the process for several days with more oil and plants until you have gotten enough.

Baths

Maintaining purity during your attempts to communicate with the spirits is also essential to practice. Baths are viewed commonly as purifying—they are meant to help to prepare you for the ritual that you intend to perform, allowing you to open your mind and spirit up. Your openness then allows you to create a means of accessing the spirit world, which is how you are able to create your petition for what you want in the first place. Really, purification baths serve a very important amplification effect that you can use for your rootwork.

However, they can also be used to break ties as well. If you have made ties that are unhealthy, unnatural, or simply just negative, you can sever those ties with the bathing process. Bonds that are negative can be dangerous. Likewise, there could be occurrences in which ancestral curses fall upon you. If this happens, you can take special baths that will help to end those curses.

Sometimes, the problem that is faced is that you have unintentionally offended someone, creating a grudge that is held against you. That grudge could be problematic if the other person is spiritual enough and could result in declarations that will harm you. Through a purification bath process, you can free yourself.

Baths are prepared through the utilization of hot water, plus the addition of herbs, plants, and other items. Some use vinegar; others may use milk or eggs. You need to create the bath while also utilizing candles to create a doorway into your bath by placing them on either end of the bathtub. By integrating water, which is commonly considered purifying in the first place, with herbs and candles, as well as potentially adding in oils, you create a potent concoction that you can use to create the effects desired.

Candles

Candles are also incredibly prevalent in many forms of magic and religion, and they work well to help to focus energy where it is needed. When you have a candle lit, you can use it to help you to focus your psychic power where you need it. As you do so, you can then begin projecting your thoughts toward the intentions. This requires you to work on meditation while also creating and manifesting the desired intention.

Candle magic helps you to gain the clarity you need. When you have the candle present, your mind is able to focus, and that allows you to focus effectively on the incantations or rituals that you have chosen to follow to complete your spell. Of course, this is where you start seeing the power of intention working for you as well. Spells can fail or go haywire if you do not have the right intentions, and because of that, you will need to focus entirely on what you are casting. This is exactly where that candle comes in.

Because the intention is ultimately what shapes the spells that you cast, you need to have that clarity of mind. You need to understand what you are doing and have that connection to the power that you are using. You need to be in sync with the elements and willpower, and that is why so many people will light that candle. The candle will help to unify the intent with the herbs and spells that you have chosen. It is only when the intention, the spell, and the energy line up that you will actually be able to cast the magic that you are looking to perform.

Candles typically are imbued with their own magic, or you can anoint them as well to help you to focus better. Either way, the purpose is the same. You are still working to gather and unify all thoughts while also building that willpower and desire that you have. You are working to unlock the power, and this works in several ways. As we will be addressing later, the colors of candles actually will shape the manifestation of your magic. Different shapes and different colors will allow you to change your conjuring, and because of that, you will need to be mindful.

Herbs and Roots

Plant matter of all kinds plays an important role in hoodoo. These were some of the most traditional methods of performing magic that existed and allowed for the manifestation of those powers that were intended. They were designed to heal, to protect, and to defend.

The purpose of your own herbs and roots are quite important. They work in all sorts of different manners to create various effects that can very clearly change the outcomes of events in the world around you. Plants and herbs in general are some of the most prevalent tools that you will see in Hoodoo, and we will be dedicating a significant amount of space later to determine the various purposes of the herbs, plants, and roots that you will be able to utilize if you want to create the intended effects. Nevertheless, plants, in general, become an essential part of Hoodoo magic, and you will need to know how to wield them.

It is often encouraged to start understanding how to grow your own herbs and plants as well. They do not need much space, especially if you grow just a few of the main ones. However, you must also make sure that you have the identification of the various herbs down, or you can wind up causing several problems for yourself. You must be able to see the differences between similar-looking plants, or you could end up attempting to conjure with the wrong plant.

Incense

Incense is commonly used in religion and, in fact, is also recommended in the Bible during prayer. In Psalm 141, you will find: "May my prayer be set before you like incense; may the lifting up of my hands be like the evening sacrifice." Further, you can find more evidence of this recommendation in Revelation 8:4, where it is written, "The smoke of the incense, together with the prayers of
God's people, went up before God from the angel's hand."

Remember, Hoodoo draws a lot of influence from Christianity—and that is obvious when looking at the utilization of incense in the practice of spells. Because a good deal of Hoodoo involves the utilization of prayers, the use of incense comes naturally as well. It is a method of honing your mind—it works to keep your focus, much like candles do. And, just like candles, there are many different options for scents and types of incense. In particular, you are likely to find resin forms of incense as well as incense sticks. More commonly, however, the resin is the preferred choice. This is especially the case for myrrh, dragon's blood, and frankincense.

Choosing out incense requires you to simply understand what the purpose of your spell that you wish to conjure is and which scents are likely to naturally associate. This means that you should once again pay special attention to the various herbs that exist, so you are choosing the ones that are the most fitting for the purposes that you are attempting to achieve. Knowing which to use will help you to ensure that at the end of the day, you will choose out the right ones.

Divination Tools

Now, divination is a topic that could fill several books on its own with ease. Divination tools are various tools that will enable you to start seeing into the future to piece together the likelihood of whatever it is that you would like to see happen. There are several different tools that are utilized for divination that all work in various ways to start spelling out the future for you before you have to do anything at all. We won't be getting into how to divine the future too much in this book just due to the sheer depth that you would need to go into. However, we will be discussing the various options that you have.

Most commonly, you see people turn to cards, bone, and candles to divine the future. When reading the cards, you are engaging in what is known as cartomancy. This is the process of reading the future through the utilization of a deck of cards. In particular, the kings and queens of the deck hold the most significance, signifying family, authorities, loved ones, and more. Through drawing the cards, you can start to understand who is being referred to in order to start piecing together what the most likely results that you will see are.

Bone reading is commonly referred to as osteomancy, and is another common form of foretelling what is to come that is featured around the world. You will need a set of bones to read the future, and the

ones the most commonly used were chicken or possum bo
traditions are rooted in West Africa and remained p
hoodoo. However, the tools for this task are a bit harder to get than simply using a deck of cards. If you are using the bones of an animal that you have found outside, you will need to clean and cure the bones, which is not always a very pleasant method. From there, you must bless them, and then you can start casting your bones. They are commonly cast by tossing them onto a table or other surface after asking a question. Horizontal bones are a yes, while vertical bones are a no.

You can also implement scrying, but this is more difficult. You would toss the bones down onto a table or other surface and then watch until you can start to discern some sort of answer out of it. By doing so, you can start figuring out the meaning. However, this is slower and typically much broader.

Candles are commonly used as well, reading the way that they burn to determine what may happen next. This is one method that we will be delving into a bit more depth. You will take a look at how long, how bright, and the colors that a flame burns to start figuring out what it is that you can expect to see in the situation that you are going into. Nevertheless, it is a powerful tool when utilized correctly, and you should pay close attention to it if you want to determine its uses accordingly.

Mojo Bags

Mojo bags refer to talismans or amulets. They are commonly described as a "prayer in a bag," referring to the fact that you will be casting your very own intentions when you utilize these bags. They are primarily for protection. However, there is more to it in hoodoo.

In hoodoo, you will also see that there is a degree of potency included that goes a step further. The mojo bag is more along the lines of a long-term spell that you can use to focus your power. It is meant to drive that power over a period of time, allowing you to create the intended result. It is meant to be tied to who you are and the fate that you will face. It is meant to keep you on track.

Mojo bags are incredibly powerful, and you must be mindful in creating them. If you are not careful, you can cause this process to not work. There is a certain degree of balance that is needed to ensure that you have the right potency, and if you fail to create it properly, you can see major repercussions. For this reason, if you do not have the skill to create your own, you can seek out those who would be able to create them for you.

These bags are used for several different purposes, but when you are in the earliest stages of hoodoo, there are just three that are really relevant to you:

1. **Activating the power of attracting your wishes:** If you are driven by a desire to see something manifest in your life, a

mojo bag can help you to make it happen. Whether that desire is for luck, love, wealth, or safety, the mojo bag can help to create a situation in which you are constantly attracting the one wish you are attempting to manifest.

2. **Protecting you:** Protection spells are incredibly potent, and as such, they require you to have immense power as well. As a beginning rootworker, you may not be able to conjure

enough, and for that reason, you can have a mojo bag as the source of power for this. The protection mojo bags are generally quite effective at maintaining the power necessary to sustain the protection.

3. **To deepen strength:** Though you may not realize it, you actually have significantly more power within you than you are accessing. You have so much information and power that has been passed down by your ancestors. That power is not always easy to access if you do not know what you are doing, but it is there for you to tap into if you want it. Your mojo bag can help you to tap into that power. You can learn to recognize the strength within yourself so you can use it rather than calling on the spirits to help.

Creating your own mojo bags is possible as well. Depending upon the intent that you have, you would gather items that are similar and that have the meaning that is intended. When you can identify what it is that you want and need in your bag, you can start to add them. Then, say an incantation that is related to what it is that you desire, and you have got your very own mojo bag that only you can use to its fullest extent.

Name Papers

One thing that you will see used regularly in hoodoo is the creation of a name paper. In fact, you will see several spells that utilize them at the end of this book. Creating name papers, obviously, becomes a very important part of any hoodoo practice, so you will need to know how to make them.

Name papers are, simply put, paper that has the name of the intended target of your spell written onto them. There are many ways that you can do this, but the simplest way will be discussed here. You want to have some sort of paper on hand for these at all times. The paper may be from a brown bag, or it could be a piece of parchment or something else that you have. But, in a pinch, any paper will work.

The key here, however, is that the paper must be torn by hand rather than cut. You want all four edges of your paper to be torn by yourself rather than cut into straight lines. This is because scissors and knives are symbolic—they are weapons. By using scissors to cut a perfect square out, you are symbolically harming the person that you intend to target with your spell. This is a huge problem if you are attempting something a bit more benign for obvious reasons, and because of that, you will want to prevent this from happening at all costs. Just tear the paper—it's better to be safe than sorry anyway.

Once you have the paper that you are using, you will want to write on the paper. You will write the other person's name, typically in an odd number. You want to write it in threes for manifestation, fives for domination, sevens for luck, and nines for enemy work.

Ideally, you will use a complete birthday as well to make your target even more specific. You want to use their whole name with their whole birthday as well. If the person is married, you should use their married last name. You want to make sure that you are using their name, however, and not a nickname.

Some people like to go further with their name papers and create them with more detail. However, for the magic that you will see in this book, the above is enough. If you wish for something with more power, you can add more to the paper, such as writing the intention of your spell clearly over the name. You would rotate the paper around 180 degrees and write directly on top of the name what you intend to manifest. If you are looking for love, for example, you might write "SOULMATE" over the name that you have written, with the word upside down compared to the name.

From there, you can also write in a circle around the name and manifestation. However, you must do so in cursive, in a clockwise manner, without ever lifting your pen or marker up. It should be some sort of intention statement. For example, you may write, "May Jane Doe finds someone who is worthy of being her partner, who will protect, love, cherish, and provide her with a happy and fulfilled life," in a circle all around the name. You will only lift your pen up when you have closed the circle, and then, after the circle has been closed, you can go back to dot and cross letters as necessary.

You can then anoint the paper with oil or with powder that is fitting to the petition that you are making. Typically, if you are adding the oil, you will do so in each corner and then put one last drop in the center of the petition to complete it. This will grant your spell the most power possible.

Then, you fold your paper. If you want to draw someone toward you, you fold toward you, then turn clockwise and fold toward you again, then repeat this one more time. You should get a small square. To banish or repel someone or something, you do the opposite—you fold away from you and rotate the paper counterclockwise instead.

CHAPTER 3: KEY ELEMENTS OF HOODOO

Most magical practices that exist depend on some sorts of elements. In particular, they bring together water, fire, earth, and air, all four of which are commonly considered to be distinctive elements that exist. Each of these elements has power in the universe, and that is recognized in Hoodoo as well. However, it is not just those elements that we see in the world that are important. There is more that is used, primarily in symbolism and in the connection to the earth that they maintain, that are important to understand as well.

In hoodoo, most of the elements that we use are those that will help us to connect to the spiritual realm. They are there to help us bridge that gap to start to communicate with the spirits. It requires a degree of symbolism, which you will start to see throughout the coming chapters. And, we will also see that the symbolism and representative magic is actually incredibly beneficial. In this chapter, you will start to see that there is some degree of elemental force that helps to interact with the spiritual realm. In being able to create that bridge by actively connecting to these elements, you will get that power. You will be able to see how the spirits tend to interact with these different elements and what you can do with them. Before you know it, you will be able to start making your own rituals and spells yourself.

Within this chapter, we will be going over several important elements.

We will be going over the spirits, the roots, the earth, and some important symbolism. We will also be addressing purifications and what you can do to ensure that you keep yourself protected as well. Through going through all of these different steps, you will start to get that power that you are looking for. You will start to see how you can communicate with the spirits and begin to influence the world around you.

Ancestral Spirits

Perhaps one of the most integral elements of Hoodoo is the ancestral spirits. We know they are there. We have them there, working with us. They are a part of us. They are the ones that came before us, and without them, we would not be here. Being able to connect to our ancestral spirits is where we draw our power. They are our roots; they are the ones whose blood courses through our veins.

Blood magic is one of the most powerful forms that exist. However, it can also be the most dangerous. Blood itself cannot be faked. It is directly related to the biology that came before you. It is directly related to the people that came before us and the biology that we share. This means that, in your blood and in your DNA, you carry your own history. We can track our roots with DNA through science, but that trail is also there spiritually.

Ancestral magic refers to the DNA that you inherited from those who came before you. It refers to the connections that you have, the essence and spirits of those who came before you. Your descendants will share that connection with you. That lineage is incredibly powerful, and when you can identify it and start to actively tap into it, you can start seeing the power that you have. However, this sort of blood magic is not without risk. There is always the chance that there is a curse that is causing you to pay for something from the past. Think of karma—you reap what you sow. Sometimes, however, your ancestors reap what you sow as well.

Someone with a terrible temper may actually have family members with terrible tempers as well. That temper was inherited in genetics. However, other traits that are a bit more intangible can also be passed down. Some people are particularly fortunate. Others may find themselves suffering from a curse. Ancestors who have done something that was so good or so bad that it impacted their descendants can create ties of blessings or curses to their blood. This power matters. While you personally may have never done anything that would warrant being treated poorly, the truth is, it is entirely possible that someone else in your past has.

Similarly, however, you have the power that is passed down. Your power that you draw on comes from your ancestors. And, if you fail to ever actively acknowledge it, you can wind up in situations that are very undesirable for you. Your power can slowly wane over time as it is not acknowledged, fizzling out until it is barely there. However, it is there, no matter what. It may not be active at the moment if you fail to use it, but the truth is, it is still there, and you can still draw from it.

Your ancestral spirits are with you at all times. They are present, and they will try to guide you if you give them a chance. If you ignore them, they may not be particularly open to you, but they are there. Remember, they are more powerful than you. They are more experienced than you. They have wisdom that they can share with you. They can help you to make choices that are going to help you, but that requires you to actually acknowledge them. That requires you to be there in positions where you can and will be able to make choices that will help you.

You have to be able to respect your ancestors and invite them into your life so you can access them when you need them. By setting aside an ancestral altar, a place where you invite and acknowledge your ancestors, you can have them present for you. You can have them present for magic, but also to guide you when you need it. You can do this with mementos or photos of those who came before you. You can acknowledge them by leaving offerings on this altar as well, and that can help you to appease them and acknowledge that they are there for you.

When you are able to start making those connections to your ancestors, you start seeing that you are capable of so much more. You start recognizing that you have that power within yourself and that you can call upon that power whenever you might need it. Before you know it, you have got that power. You are going to be able to call upon your ancestors when you need them, and they will be there for you if you have given them that connection to you and you have begun to honor them as well.

Spirits of the Roots

Hoodoo is known as rootwork, thanks to the fact that the bulk of the power of what you do will be connected to the plants, roots, and herbs that you use. They will help you to focus on. They will help you to start channeling your power where you need it. These herbs are meant to be beneficial spiritually and physically as well, and many of these herbs also serve very medicinal purposes. As you will start to see in the next chapter, there are many different options based upon the powers and properties of each plant that you can see.

Remember that, once upon a time, we didn't have a bottle of Tylenol we could take to cure our headaches—we had herbs. We didn't have law enforcement to call and serve a restraining order to protect us— we had our spiritual guides, ancestral spirits, and the rituals that we could perform to try to sway the fate of the world so we could be protected. This is imperative to remember.

We have always found ways to figure out what we need. We have always known that the Earth provided us with a way that we could heal our bodies, and we turned to the Earth to provide us with guidance in other ways as well. The plants that were around us were there to help us. Some were even able to help us bridge that gap and connect with the spirit world. By learning which plants will help you to bridge that gap, you can start reaching out to the spirits to ensure that you have that help.

Being able to know which plants will help us to create the effects that we need or desire will help us to become more powerful. It will help us to be able to get those effects that we want. From being able to cast protection to be able to draw luck or goodwill, we start to see that we have that power to do what we needed. We start to know which roots will do what and how that can help us to be able to cast the spells that we seek to get the effects that we need.

Spirits of the Earth

There are also spirits of the Earth that must be acknowledged as well. We are not just drawing from our ancestors and the roots that we've chosen—we are also drawing from the spirits of the Earth. By drawing soil or other earth from the ground of locations, you can start to create the effect that you want. The soil that you choose will have the properties of the place that you drew it from. A bank, for example, would bring about wealth. A casino may bring luck. A courthouse may bring justice, and earth from a crime scene may evoke evil. The earth that we use can help us to ground our spells—it works to start focusing and balancing out the magic that we draw from.

Because magic is so incredibly powerful, it can be volatile as well. However, being able to stop and connect that to the Earth helps you to make sure that it is more focused. Adding soil can also help you to hone the spell that you are using. Adding that soil can actually help you to direct the spell to where you want it to go as well. The love spell that you might want to work on could be more focused if you used soil from somewhere good to help hone it. The spell for justice might be better if you add in the soil from the courthouse that you will be in. These nuances will help to protect you; they help to guide the power that you are drawing from so you know that it will go the direction that you want. This will be enough to help you successfully navigate these different situations that you are in.

The Earth also brings with it more as well. It brings with it the wealth of the universe as well. Think about it—gold comes from the Earth. Gemstones come from the Earth. The world around us is surrounded by this need for energy, and when you draw from it, you start to attract wealth as well.

However, you must remember that you have to be selective about where you get your soil or earth. If you were to take it from the desert, you would be attracting a barren wasteland. This may not be what you need if you are going for a fertility spell. Rather, you should be turning your attention to places that will be representative of fertility as well, such as a farm field or a garden. This helps you to draw those fertile properties to ensure that at the end of it all, you will get that effect that you are looking for.

Graveyards

When you consider that one of the primary factors used in Hoodoo is ancestral spirits, it should come as no surprise that you will also be working in graveyards. Now, working in graveyards is not exactly a beginner's tactic, but it is a key part of hoodoo. It requires a high degree of intuition and focuses because when you enter, there may be spirits there that are not pleased that you are there. They may not be there to help you, and that can become dangerous for you as well.

There are spirits that would prefer to be left alone or would prefer to lead you astray. As a beginner, it would be better for you to focus on your time at home. Learn to develop your skills with the ancestral altar and use that before you start delving into graveyards, which are going to be dangerous for you. Eventually, when you have got that spiritual intuition and that experience with your ancestors, you can start trying to experiment with graveyards, but do not do so lightly.

Before we delve further into discussing graveyards, however, remember that graveyards are not evil. They are not negative, either. They are actually, in hoodoo, believed to be highly revered. Rather than being places of grief and sadness, they are regarded as places of reverence. After all, in hoodoo, you are acknowledging that death is not final. Death is not the end of everything—rather, it is the beginning of the next phase. Your ancestors have died; they are no longer walking on this earth in their physical forms, but they still exist. They are still there, and their energy is still prevalent if you know where you are looking or what you need. If you can understand this concept, you start to step away from those negative connotations that the graveyard may initially evoke. Yes, you leave the bodies of your loved ones behind in them. However, their energy lives on.

We acknowledge that the graveyard becomes a place where we can access the energies of our loved ones. Death is that connection between our world and the next one, and because of that, the graveyard becomes symbolic of that journey.

The graveyard, then, creates the effect of evoking transitions. It is the beginning and the end at the same time. Graveyard earth can be that perfect way to harness the energy that you need to be representative of that end or beginning. It can help to end eras or times. However, it can also be used to create new beginnings.

Remember, however, that when you do take earth from a grave, you need to pay attention to where you are. You need to be selective of the people whose graves you take from. If you were to choose the wrong graves, you could end up creating issues with your spells. And, if you are not respectful, you can actually cause other issues as well.

Collecting graveyard dirt must be very respectful and almost even formal at times. You want to make sure that you are to only choose the right grave, paying attention to the energy that you wish to evoke, but you must also appease the spirit that resides there. You need to be respectful of their resting place ad you should either pay for the soil with some pennies or with some whiskey or something else. This helps to show them that you are thanking them for the soil.

There are different ways that you can choose out a grave to draw from a spirit. From being able to figure out what the power of that spirit is through divination to using your own intuition after you have gotten the experience necessary, you can start figuring out what you are doing with ease. Walk around the graveyard that you are in. Start taking the time to figure out what you are doing and to get a feel for where you are at. Get to know the spirits. You may find some that draw you, and if you do feel compelled to approach one, remember that you should do your research.

Remember that with this kind of magic, however, you are not just trying to get something. You are making relationships. You are building that connection with the energy of another being that was also once alive. You are not just trying to buy their services with a splash of whiskey or a few bites of something. You are trying to create that relationship so you can rely upon the people that you are connected to.

Crossroads

Crossroads also represent an important element to Hoodoo magic. In particular, when we see crossroads, we acknowledge that there is an opportunity. Think about it—when you stand at the center of a crossroads, you can see that there are four different directions you can go. You have opportunities, and those opportunities that present themselves are incredibly powerful as well.

You can use these to start casting off bad energy. You can use them to protect yourself and to create the effect of encouraging transition. However, unlike a graveyard, a crossroads doesn't have to carry that same air of death that you would otherwise see.

Additionally, the crossroads represents a place of magical neutrality. This makes it commonplace for your spell remnants to be disposed of. If you have created a spell using supplies that is very magically powerful, you may want to neutralize the power in the remnants by leaving them at a crossroads. This will help to lower the power that they have so that they can be disposed of safely.

Generally speaking, if you are going to perform spells that utilize a crossroads, you want to go either late at night or very early in the mornings. By doing so, you can get the fullest effect that you are looking for.

Purifications

Just about every magical practice is going to have purification and cleansing necessary in it. They will require you to find ways to keep the energy pure and focused. In Hoodoo, this helps you to ensure that you are ready to approach the spell. It helps you to ensure that you are able to practice well and open yourself to the power that you are looking for. Ritual cleansing becomes imperative if you want to practice, and if you were to study underneath a teacher, they would teach you how to cleanse and purify before they would teach you anything else.

When you choose to start a spell, you have to start with that cleanse. It helps you to ensure that you are in the right headspace to be able to perform the spell that you want to. It helps to ensure that at the end of the day, you will not be allowing any negativity to erode on what you are trying to do. In purifying your mind, body, and spirit, you ensure that you are in a position where you will be able to better approach the world and those in it. You create the effect where you are able to bring your attention to where you need it.

A spiritual cleanse will help you to ensure that you remove any negativity or negative energy. When you are cleansed, you are in the right physical and mental mindset to create the effects that you need. It will help you to be cleaned emotionally and mentally, and that means that your spell is less likely to be interfered with by outside forces.

With the right tools for yourself, you can make sure that you are entirely cleansed, and when you create that cleanse, you will open yourself up to the spiritual energy around you. You will be able to access the spells and the power that you need to ensure that you are capable of the effects that you are looking for.

The cleanses that you choose to use will vary greatly. Some rituals will involve a bathing process. Others work just fine with the use of herbs and potions that you rub onto your body. The effect is typically quite rapid, and you will start feeling the effects almost immediately. Keep in mind that the cleanses that you do use will be highly dependent upon what kinds of effects you are looking for. From being able to create a love spell to be able to fend off any negative or evil energy, you will need to follow a different process, and you must make sure that your cleanses are at the right time of day as well.

Cleanses tend to be done prior to the sun rising but must also be done after waking up. This means that if you are going to cleanse yourself, you will need to wake up early and then cleanse yourself. You must make sure that you avoid speaking to people, too. You cannot speak to others before cleansing yourself. Of course, this means that before you can do anything at all, you will need to be mindful of the timing that you choose for everything. You must make sure that you plan ahead before you start a spell, so you leave that opening for cleansing and purifying.

CHAPTER 4: ROOTWORK

Rootwork is one of the most basic, fundamental practices that you will find in Hoodoo. The role of plants will come up again and again, and you will see this in just about every spell you ever attempt to conjure. Thanks to the powers of the various herbs and plants, you will see that magic can be created all around you. Remember, certain spirits will inhabit certain plants, and thanks to the doctrine of signatures, each plant will have its own attributes to alter the flow of the magic that you are creating.

Dubious? Do not be—every culture in the world has recognized the power of plants. They have been turned to as healing since the ancient days before medicine became as industrialized as it is now. Medicine in the form that we know it today did not exist, but plants were there, and people would commonly use those plants to heal. They would also use those plants to purify and to protect as well. Hoodoo draws from these principles as well and allows for the creation of the magical effects that you are looking for.

Within this chapter, we are delving right into this concept. We are taking a look more thoroughly into the idea of what rootwork is, why it is so integral, and how it appears in the various forms of hoodoo. You will see rootwork and work with plants throughout the book, making this chapter an important step in building the foundation of knowledge that you will need. In particular, as you reach the end of this chapter, you will get a guide to the most common plants that you are likely to encounter to help you to understand precisely what it is that you are going to need.

Rootwork is literally working with the plants around you. Now, you may no longer live where your ancestors are from and, therefore, may no longer have that access to the same plants. However, many of them can be purchased online to be shipped to you, or you may be able to grow them yourself indoors. Either way, rootwork will offer you that special connection to your history. It will grant you protection and help you to tap into the power of your ancestors as well to ensure that you are safe.

Using Plants in Hoodoo

Remember that in hoodoo, the starting point is always the intention. Your intention matters here, as well. Do you intend to conjure regularly? Do you wish to have that power to practice again and again? If so, you must understand how plants work, how they grow and recognize their power. It is strongly recommended that any Hoodoo practitioner grows their own garden to begin connecting to the plants. When you have fresh herbs to pick, the connection to the Earth is much stronger than when you purchase dried plants from the store. Sometimes, you simply do not have the plant needed, or sometimes, you cannot access it natively, and that is okay. Purchased plants can still help you to achieve your goals. However, what you are looking for more than ever is that connection to nature and the spirits that inhabit it. You need that connection to the world, and that is something that is gained through the gardening process. Through working the soil, growing your own plants from a seed to harvest, and through nurturing it at all stages, you are lovingly creating your own intention into the plant. You are putting some of your own energy into your plants.

Now, you might protest and say that you do not have space—but remember this, you do not need much space to grow your own herbs, and you can actually do so just about anywhere. Even on your wall, you could hang planters to get some vertical space if you are short on it otherwise. You can grow them in just about anything, but one thing is for sure: You will have them available to you immediately if you can grow them yourself.

Most people start off growing sage, rosemary, and mint. These are three of the most commonly used herbs that you are likely to need, and they are incredibly simple to grow as well. Sage, in particular, is cleansing in nature—it will allow you to build up the power that you are looking for through simply providing you with a means to purify the space that you are in.

If you do not want to grow the herbs yourself, consider working with someone local to you that is growing their own herbs for their own Hoodoo purposes. Typically, those who grow for magical reasons know what they need to do and are able to actually empower their plants by paying special attention to the moon cycle as they grow them while also harvesting at just the right time. When you purchase at the store, you still have herbs that will work for basic spells, but they may not have that same degree of power.

Creating your spells from your plants, then, becomes a bit of a mixand-match process. However, you must still be mindful. Certain plants do not mix well with others, and energies can class, nullify, or create the wrong intended effect. You need to remember that not all plants will work well so you do not end up getting yourself into unintended trouble, something which can be detrimental to your own success in conjure. Nevertheless, this process is a learning process, and through reading through the rest of this chapter, you will start to get an idea of the powers that you can achieve in nature.

Plants to Remember

The plants that you will see listed here are incredibly powerful. They each have their own specific properties that lend themselves to various processes and spells. Some are good for purifying. Others lend themselves to protection or luck. Others still may be used to encourage love, lust, or even fertility. Remember, the origins of rootwork were for people who had a very little degree of control over their lives, so they found a way to achieve what they wanted in other ways—primarily through plants instead. By turning to the plants of the world, they were able to take back control. They could influence their fates more than they otherwise would have been able to, and they learned over time which plants were good for which purposes.

The information that you see here in front of you is that which has been gathered and tested for generations. It is incredibly powerful and will aid you in ensuring that no matter what it is that you choose to do, you have got the power to influence the world around you. You have that degree of control that you will need to help yourself, and because of that, you should take the time to learn it. So, let's get started with several common plants that you will utilize during your time practicing Hoodoo.

Agrimony

This plant is used to reverse jinxes, hexes, curses, and spells. It is meant to aid in the ability to overcome fear or anything that is holding us up. It helps to dispel negativity and is commonly used as a wash or oil for healing rituals or in spell work to bring out the truest feelings.

Alfalfa

Alfalfa is a strong ingredient that is used for bringing wealth or material goods. It is kept at home to ensure that you have food and money or in the wallet while meeting with bankers.

Alkanet

This root is used as a dye. In magic, it is used to aid in monetary matters or those regarding business. It can also be used as a countermeasure against people who may be actively attempting to hinder your financial success.

Allspice

These berries are carried by those looking for money through gambling.

Althea

Althea is believed to increase psychic power while drawing good spirits. It is also commonly used in rituals of protection. Also commonly known as marshmallow leaf.

Angelica root

This is considered a guardian plant and will bring upon the power of the angels. It is known to give strength to women and is commonly used to either protect children, ward of evil, or to provide luck to one in the realms of health and family.

Barberry root

This root is commonly placed in the path of enemies to reduce the effect those enemies have. It is a common root found in protection amulets and may also be referred to as "holy thorn." It can free you from the power someone else holds over you.

Bearberry

Bearberry is sometimes referred to as "uva ursi." It is usually ingested as a tea to increase psychic power.

Black mustard seed

This is used to interfere with baneful magic against you. It confuses the mind of the enemy. Simply sprinkle it where enemies will walk. It is sometimes referred to as "seed of strife and discord."

Black walnut

This is commonly used to allow for astral travel. It can also be used for hexing or breakup work.

Blue flag root

Blue flag root is common in money and prosperity look. You will see it sometimes referred to as "snake lily," and it is used to create incense that is burned to bring money.

Boneset

Boneset is commonly used by creating infusions that are sprinkled around the home. This helps to fend off any evil spirits that may be hanging around your home. It is directly used for helping to protect the health or undoing any magic that was used to negatively impact your health.

Buckeye

Buckeye is carried due to the power it has to bring you luck and money. It is also used somewhat in divination as well. It is meant to provide that sort of luck, and it is said to keep you in "pocket money." Some choose to turn to buckeye to use as a charm for male fertility, while others may choose to use it to rub the buckeye before rolling dice.

Burdock root

The root of burdock is typically used by stringing it onto a necklace and then using it for protection. It is both potent in protecting and cleansing, and some also choose to carve large roots into amulets that are used to fend off any negative energy.

Calamus root

This is used to dominate or control other people, to essentially bend their will to whatever you wanted from them.

Calendula

This is used for the protection of all kinds. It is commonly put into wreaths to place above doors or to protect the home. Some also use it for winning court cases.

Cascara sagrada bark

If you have got a legal battle coming up and do not know if you will win it, you will probably turn to cascara sagrada bark. By creating an infusion and surrounding your property before your court case, you will help to protect yourself. Or, you can also burn it on charcoal the day before your case to up your chances of victory.

Catnip

Catnip is commonly used in love and attraction spells that are meant to catch the heart of others. It is also commonly used in spells of beauty and happiness.

Chamomile

Chamomile is used for bringing sleep and meditation but can also be quite protective. You can use it to remove spells that have been cast on you, or you can use it to attract money to your life. It is a favorite of gamblers.

Chewing John

Sometimes referred to as "Little John," this is commonly used to help with legal or court casework.

Chicory

Chicory is commonly relied on to remove obstacles in your life. If you are struggling to achieve your dreams, a bit of chicory carried with you can help. It can also aid in gaining favors from other people or to unlock inner strength and other powers. It is meant to make one invulnerable and successful.

Cinnamon chips

Cinnamon chips are commonly used to bring money into your life. Burning it as incense can also help as protection. It may be used to bring luck, create protection, for consecration, and for divination.

Coltsfoot

Coltsfoot is typically found in spells that are meant to trigger peace. It is sometimes burned as an incense to increase psychic powers and to clear away foggy thoughts.

Comfrey

Comfrey is meant to keep the wealth that you already have. It can also be used in travel to ensure that you do not lose your bagging. In the car, it can help you drive without accidents as well. It is known to fend off evil from strangers and also to protect you from having things stolen.

Damiana

This herb is considered useful in increasing the degree of passion or to trigger a spark that has faded away. It is used commonly in sexuality or lust magic.

Dandelion root

Dandelion root is known to promote higher levels of psychic power or tot rigger the sending of telepathic messages. It is commonly used in dream pillows to protect one during sleep, in divination or when calling the spirits to your aid.

Dixie John

Dixie John root is also sometimes called "Low John" or "Southern John." It is used for matters involving family or love and also is used to enhance one's sex life. It can also be used against people who threaten your marriage.

Dog grass root

This is sometimes called "couch grass." It is commonly used to bring in lovers but can also be used to break up people. It is usually found in candles and in doll babies.

Elecampane

Elecampane is regularly used with both mistletoe and vervain to create love powders. It is also believed to protect against witches when combined with mugwort and nettle.

Fennel

Fennel is regularly hung in both doors and windows to protect the home from any bad spirits. It also works well when you hold it with yourself. It can prevent curses while also increasing levels of confidence and courage.

Fenugreek

Fenugreek is known for being useful in money-drawing spells and mixtures. It could bring money as well if you were to use seeds in mop water.

Five finger grass

This is known to bring good luck for both money and love. If you are going to ask someone for something, bring some five finger grass with you. It can also fend off evil or to remove hexes.

Ginger

Ginger root is regularly used for spells meant to bring achievement or success. It is also known to boost the power of spells if you chew ginger root before your ritual.

Grains of paradise

This is commonly used to boost protection and good luck. It may also be used if you are seeking a job or if you have a wish to make. Carrying these grain in your pocket during interviews is said to boost your chances of success.

Gravel root

Gravel root is turned to for aiding in finding new work. It is recommended to be carried when applying for jobs or for asking for a raise. It can also be used to alleviate tension in the home.

Hibiscus

Hibiscus is regularly used for both love and marriage spells, commonly consumed as tea. It may also be used to boost sexual attraction, clairvoyant energy or to attract good spirits while simultaneously repelling evil ones.

High John conqueror root

This is regularly added to mojo bags and is used for power, money, strength, luck, masculine energy, and more. It is great for boosting potion strengths too. By washing your hands with an infusion of High John, you will up your chances of winning in gambling.

Honeysuckle

Honeysuckle flowers are used to bind your love interest to you. When you infuse honeysuckle into oil, you can use it to anoint foreheads to boost psychic vision. It can also be used in candles.

Hops

Hops are regularly used in dream magic to boost the power of visions during sleep. It is also used to fight off nightmares and to promote peaceful sleep.

Hyssop

Hyssop is used to unhex, and is commonly added to spiritual baths to remove curses and hexes. It is also regularly used for purification and cleansing. When it is hung inside of your home, it can also help to push out negativity and evil.

Jasmine flower

When you use the jasmine flower, you boost your love magic. It can also bring about newer ideas and prophetic dreams. You can often also use jasmine to attract your soul mate.

Lavender

Lavender is a commonly used flower for friendship or harmony. It is commonly used in love spells but also in boosting friendship bonds. It can also be beneficial to use in sleep and rest to help to center the mind. If you want to attract someone new or to protect yourself from a cruel spouse, you can wear lavender. It can also be used for healing or purification.

Lemon balm

You can use lemon balm to aid in soothing emotional pain, such as healing after the end of a relationship. It can aid in calming the mind of those with mental health issues and can also be used for focus and clarity, such as before meditation.

Lemon peel

Lemon peels can be made into a tea that can be used as a cleansing wash for ritual tools or new items that you have purchased. It can also remove the old to make space for the new.

Lemongrass

Lemongrass was cleansing spiritually and used regularly. It can help to remove jinxes or to clean out residual energy that was left in a home or business that you have just bought. It can also clean ritual tools or amulets as well.

Licorice root

This is commonly used for love and lust magic as well as for maintaining fidelity. It can also be used to control other people. It is commonly used in spells that trigger others to follow you. It can also help you to take control and dominate others or situations.

Lily of the valley

Lily of the valley is known to be healing while also boosting peace and tranquility. It can also be used to end any harassment that you have been suffering from. It can also be used to encourage the longevity of marriage while also encouraging peace and comfort. However, do not ingest it.

Lovage

Lovage is used to encourage attractiveness. It is also used to infuse into oils to anoint candles of attraction. It may also be used for encouraging psychic dreaming or to purify.

Mandrake root

Mandrake root is usually used to protect the home when placed above a mantle. It is also said to be used to repel demons. It is commonly used tied to a doll baby to bind love to you. It can also have a dollar bill wrapped around it to encourage money.

Mullein

This is occasionally used round and then used instead of graveyard dirt. It may also be hung over doorways to protect against demons and evil spirits. It may also protect against nightmares.

Nettle

Nettle is regularly used as a protector. It is meant to break jinxes while also sending it back to the caster. It may also be worn as a talisman or used in baths.

Peony root

Peony is regularly used to bring in good fortune while also protecting against negative energy. It can be worn to protect yourself from evil, or it can be used to guard the home as well. As a necklace, it can protect children or can be used as a way to exorcise homes.

Peppermint

Peppermint is used for both healing and purification. It can be used as a rub or wash, or it could be used to expel negative energy as well. If you want to protect your home against illness, spread some peppermint around.

Plantain

Plantain is perfect for healing, protection, and strength. It is sometimes also called snakeweed due to the fact that it is believed to ward off snakes. It can also be used to fend off both death and sickness as well.

Queen Elizabeth root

Sometimes referred to as Orris root, this root is commonly used to attract men. It is also used to encourage popularity, communication, and success in your endeavors.

Red clover

Red clover is used for marriage while also encouraging a good sex life. It can be used in baths to encourage money, financial success, success, and luck. And, with the use of red clover, you can remove evil spirits as well.

Red pepper flakes

Red pepper flakes are commonly used in enemy work. If you want to fight off someone, you can sprinkle the red pepper in the path of your nemesis.

Rose petals

Rose petals are commonly used to trigger dreams of the love that you will have in the future. It is commonly used for all sorts of love spells to encourage a long-lasting relationship.

Rue

Rue is powerful in protection and is usually used to craft talismans.

You can also add some around your home to protect it.

Sage leaf

In hoodoo, you specifically want rubbed sage leaf—the kind that is grown in the garden rather than white sage. It is then crushed and used to burn and cleanse and purify areas. It can also help with courage and strength.

Sarsaparilla

This is used in love spells as well as money spells. It can also be used to encourage health or for house blessings. When you use it in spells, you can prolong your life, sexuality, and passion. It is also used to encourage virility.

Senna

You can use this to draw in the love of strangers or to encourage love.

Valerian root

This is used to encourage peace while also ending quarrels. Sometimes, you can use it to replace graveyard dirt as well. It can also be used in darker magic as well.

Violet leaf

Violet leaf is used to calm the nerve and encourages visions and prophetic dreams and visions. It also stimulates creativity while also promoting peace. Violet leaf also provides protection from evil while also being used for love and romance.

Wormwood

This is also commonly called absinthe. It is used to increase psychic powers for divination purposes. It can also be used for scrying and prophecy as well. It is also used to encourage protection. Occasionally used to burn with mugwort to encourage helpful spirits. It is also said to aid in preventing accidents and can be used for exorcism.

Yarrow

Yarrow is used to encouraging healing, self-esteem, defeating fear, and encouraging courage as well. It is usually used in ritual baths to boost psychic abilities or end curses.

CHAPTER 5: CANDLE MAGIC AND CONJURE OILS

In hoodoo, both candles and oils will be used heavily. Both of these are designed to help you to focus your energy. They help to create amplifiers for the spells that you are choosing out, and through using them effectively, you can ensure that your spells are much more effective than they otherwise would be. This means that if you need an added boost to your spell, you want it in one of these forms.

Most spells will utilize one of these, and you will need to know how to use them accordingly. This is why we will be taking the time to go through how to use candle magic and conjure oils to ensure that you understand what you are doing, how you will do it, and why. Think of this chapter as a guide to recognizing these two powerful aspects of spiritual magic that you can use to cast your own spells effectively and thoroughly.

A Guide to Candle Magic

Candles are incredibly common in Hoodoo, and you will use them regularly, either in spells on their own, or used alongside other important elements, such as roots and oils, to help boost them more. Candles allow you to focus your energy. You will be honing that psychic energy that you have, pushing yourself further, and helping yourself to figure out what you are doing and open yourself up to that spiritual energy that you will need.

Most spells ad will begin with candles, especially in the earlier parts of them. The light ad glow helps you to meditate ad focus ad project those thoughts and intentions that you have and want to sharpen. This means that you should be able to use these powers to benefit yourself further. They will help you to focus your mind and push past the confusion or negativity that you might be feeling, granting you that chance to be the person that you want to be.

Using candle magic

Using candle magic requires you to focus. It requires you to be able to pay close attention to one thing at one point in time, but that is something that is incredibly difficult to do on your own. Focusing your mind on just one thing for an extended period of time to allow you to cast those spells is not always easy, but when you have a candle, you can start encouraging it. You can cut the amount of time that it will take for you to focus, and that means that you can start working on your spells sooner. Think about it—if time is of the essence, you will probably want yourself to figure out what you are doing sooner. You will probably want to pull that focus as soon as possible, and that requires you to start somewhere.

To use candle magic, you must be able to focus on the candle. You must be able to essentially meditate on it. You want to focus on the effects that the candle has, and you want to use that to build your focus. Before you know it, you will be candle-savvy in no time. But, to do so, you have to pick out the right candles as well. You must know what it is that you really want and how you can encourage that focus and development of what you need.

Candle colors

The candles that you choose will not only have their own unique shapes that matter, they also have their own individual colors. Colors actually matter immensely. The colors that you choose will help to influence the spell that you are attempting to cast, and sometimes, you will have spells that will have very specific colors that are needed. If you are casting your own spell, you might need to choose a color that is going to be suitable for you, and that requires you to know which colors mean what and how you can start putting them together. Let's go over those colors and their purposes now.

Black

Black candles are typically assumed to be evil, but the truth is, they aren't. Yes, they have a use when using magic that is going to be darker in nature, and yes, they are likely to show up in practicing the occult, but in hoodoo, they have a more benign use. They represent protection and are prevalent in protection spells. If you need to dominate others, you would also draw upon black spells.

Blue

Blue candles are those that are meant to sharpen your communication skills. They work well to ensure that you have health and healing as well, and they are perfect for meditation. If you need some clarity in your communication with your ancestors, these candles can help greatly.

Green

Green candles tend to evoke powers of money and growth. The growth aspect is also typically linked to fertility and luck. If you are looking for growth, abundance in the universe, or luck, you probably want to turn to a green candle to create those effects.

Red

Red candles are passionate and commonly used to encourage passionate feelings. In particular, red is focused on both love and revenge. These two uses may seem like they are opposing, but they are both driven by intense emotions. Red itself is strongly capable of creating those effects of riling up emotions and is able to help do exactly that. If you need passion in a spell, you probably want a red candle.

Silver

Silver candles create a sort of feminine energy, as well, as energy, is drawn from the moon. These are perfect if you need moonlight but cannot wait until you have access to it.

White

White is commonly believed to be purifying and protective. It is also a peaceful color that you can use to create a sense of calmness that you might need in a spell. It is the most common color when you are following through with incantations and spells, and it will create a degree of clarity to your thoughts that you might not have otherwise.

For cleansing and for protection, this is the perfect candle color to go to.

Yellow

Yellow candles are highly positive and are used in ways that are meant to boost morale. They are perfect for building positive emotions up, even when there are problems or stressors. It is used to evoke happiness and clarity in other people.

Reading candles

When you have your candles lit, you can then begin to draw on the energy that they create. You can start figuring out the reactions that you are trying to read so you can start recognizing the right ways to interpret the energy that is in front of you. This can start getting very deep very quickly, but if you want to know the basics, there are three key aspects to watch on your candle. You want to look at the color of your fire, the movement of your fire, and the brightness of your fire. Each of these will provide you with an understanding of what you are doing and how you are going to be able to understand them.

Color

The color that your flame takes is very indicative of the powers surrounding you. Your candle may be blue in the center all the way to read at the tip, and there is usually yellow and orange between them. Blue flames in the center show the presence of something benign or even friendly. It could be an ancestral spirit that you are aware of, or it could be an angel. The blue is good. Red, o the other hand, shows that there may be something very powerful nearby. The power could swing either way—being good or bad—and you will need to trust your intuition there. Yellow and orange help you to see the amount of energy present in the spell that you are working on.

Movement

When your candles are burning, they will typically flicker and move in the direction of the air currents. You will see the flames moving along with the current. However, if you notice that it is flickering and you are somewhere that should have air that is still, you should pay close attention. You want to look at the direction that the flame is going so you can interpret the strength and status of your spell.

Flames moving to the east tend to indicate mental soundness. Flames facing west tend to show that there is an emotion I the spell. Flames moving to the north show some degree of physicality ad flames to the south show that you have intent in your spell.

Brightness

Brightness also helps you to start seeing what is going on around you. Flames that burn low tend to mean that there are low levels of energy present in the spell as well. The flames that are higher and brighter mean that there is more energy. However, if there are flames burning unevenly, you should be mindful of focus—your spell is burning without being grounded.

The most desirable state for your candle to be in is a state in which the flame burns slowly and steadily, flickering strongly without being rapid or uneven. Steady and even means that your spell is proceeding accordingly.

A Guide to Conjure Oils

Conjure oils are regularly used in Hoodoo as well, and they have also been found in just about all religions as a form of accelerant. They work to allow you to seal a spell somewhere or to accelerate the power of it, meaning that you are accentuating those abilities and powers so they can be used further. This is essential in spells as it can be useful to bind the effects of what you want to a specific object, charm, bag, or place. You want to be able to figure out how you can ensure that the effects that you are looking for are locked into a place where you want them so you can be certain that your spell goes accordingly.

In hoodoo, conjure oils are typically extracted from plants, so they can be used to bind the essence of the plant to something else. By being able to do so, you should be able to get the effects you need. You just have to know which kinds of herbs and essences you need and where you should bind them. It is really quite simple, and if you were to follow the processes that you need, you'd see that you have got these abilities.

Using conjure oils

Using oils and powders, in some cases, is relatively simple. You will use them to anoint and dress. This allows you to start attracting the energy that you are looking for. For example, if you want to attract luck into your home, you may use powders and oils on your doorway to invite the luck in. This would work to allow luck to filter through the door.

Powders, in particular, work a bit differently. If you want to use an oil on someone but cannot get close enough to do so, simply using a powder in places where they are likely to step and then making sure that you bind the right intent to the powder in the first place, you should be able to get the effects that you are going for. This is crucial if you want to have that power over someone else. When they step on the powder, if you have done your job right, the powder will bind to their imprint, which then allows you to bind to their essence. The spell will then be focused accordingly.

Oils are tackier than powders and work a bit differently. Oils work well if you are anointing items that will not be damaged by them, or they are used to allow you to dress a candle or a mojo bag. These work well to ensure that you get the energy into the item that you are trying to attach it to, and oils actually stick longer than the powders would.

CHAPTER 6: SIMPLE SPELLS FOR LOVE

Most people crave love. They want to be blessed with that close relationship with someone else in the world, and they are willing to do whatever it will take to get it. Most people find love through trial and error. They work hard to get it by meeting people and by trying to date others. But, sometimes, that is not enough. Sometimes, those dates will not help you to find true love. You may also end up with many, many more errors than trials.

If you have suffered from your love life, repeatedly trying to find ways that you can connect to the people in your life that you want to be around, then do not fret—you can cast a spell or two to help yourself to figure out who your Mr. or Mrs. Right is. Finding that person doesn't have to be intimidating or dreaded. You can figure out the right person by casting a spell and putting your intentions out into the world. You can address the people around you. You can reach out to your ancestors and get their guidance as well. Or, you can aim for a certain person to be attracted to you, too. Either way, you are giving yourself a gift: The gift of love.

In this chapter, we're going to be taking a look at some simple love spells that will help you to connect to your loved one. We will work on attracting love, attracting someone in particular, and winning back an ex. Before you know it, you will have your own list of spells that you can turn to if you need them.

Now, you might be wondering if this is safe or fair to be doing to the people in the world. Is it really love if you have to compel someone else to love you? Are they really the right person for you if it is magic that brings them into your life? The answer here is that while you are influencing other people, they still have their own willpower. You are not making them love you—you are giving them the opportunity to love you. What they do with that opportunity is up to them, not you. What they choose to do is entirely dependent upon themselves and how they treat the world around them. They may choose to pursue you, or they may choose not to. And remember, if you are uncomfortable with creating your own love spells or trying to conjure up the effects you want, you can always choose to pass on these spells entirely.

Remember this, however—the spells that you cast need to be done tactfully. And, if you notice that a spell is not working, rather than seeing it as a sign that your magic was flawed, remember that it could be the case that they do not love you. Remember that there are no truly guaranteed outcomes with Hoodoo—you are simply influencing those around you into doing whatever it is that you are looking for them to do. You cannot force them to love you.

You should also be mindful of the kinds of people you are addressing as well. You must make sure that you are choosing out people who are good candidates for what you want. You must make sure that you are avoiding the addictive types of people out there or those with a history of mental health issues. They simply do not make very good people target with love spells.

The Come My Way Orange

This spell will help you to make your own personal energy more enticing. You are working to make yourself more likely to attract someone who will be right for you. This helps to bring in NEW love to your life rather than finding love with old sparks. To complete this spell, you will need:

- One orange

- One rose

- Nine pins

- Red thread

- Hair

- "Look Me Over" oil

Then, you just follow a few simple steps to get the effects. Before you know it, you will have some new love in your life.

1. Cut a hole into your orange, cutting out some space inside of it.

2. Take your hair and anoint it with oil. Then, repeat this with the pins and the thread.

3. First, put the hair into the rose. Then, push the rose into the orange. Using the pins, close up the hole in the orange. Then, take your red thread and use it to wrap between the pins to hold it all together.

4. Take the entire orange and rose and bury them near your home. This will start bringing new romantic partners your way!

Marry Me Packet Spell

Do you have someone that you really want to marry? Are you sure that you've found the one, but you do not know how to win them over? That may mean that this spell is precisely what you will need. This spell will help you to implant the idea of marriage into the mind of your loved one, and then, all you will have to do is wait for the magic to work! This spell will need a few simple things:

- Angelica root

- Red onion skin

- Red thread

- Magnolia leaves

- Name paper

Then, when you have everything gathered up, all you will have to do is follow these simple steps:

1. Begin by folding the roots and your onion skin into the paper.

2. Wrap up the name paper into your magnolia leaves.

3. Wrap the whole thing up in a thread.

4. Hang your packet over the door of your intended spouse's home (this may be your own if you live together) and wait for the magic to take effect!

Peaceful Love Candle Spell

Are your relationships struggling right now? Is your marriage on the rocks? Are you stressed out and wish that you could go back to those easier days when your relationship was easier? Relationships are difficult, that's for sure, but with this candle spell, you can help yourself to bring peace and prosperity back into your marriage. Before you know it, you will find your relationship getting back on track, and all you have to do is work with this candle magic to soothe those wounds between yourself and your partner. To complete this spell, you will need:

- 1 Blue 7-Day candle

- Lavender essential oil

- Sugar

- Vanilla

Then, you will follow a few simple steps to get that magic flowing!

1. Take your candle and create three small holes in the top.

2. In each of your holes, put a small amount of each ingredient. Each hole should now have oil, vanilla, and sugar placed within them.

3. Pray Psalms 45 and 46.

4. Light your candle and burn in an area of your home that is shared, such as the living room or bedroom.

5. When the candle is done burning, wash out the glass with running water, and recycle.

Always on Their Mind Bag

Need a little something to remind your lover to keep you on their mind? This is an easy little bag that you can put together to burn the passions for you in your partner's mind. You can use this on your own, making it using your lover's hair, or you can make one yourself for them. This spell is incredibly simple. You will need:

- Magnolia petals

- Red bag

- Bay leaves

- Adam and Eve roots

- Hair from your lover

- Churchyard soil

Then, you will follow these simple steps to ensure that your partner keeps you at the forefront of their minds.

1. First, put the dirt from the church into the red bag. Then, pray your lover's name over it. Repeat the prayer nine times.

2. Take the hair and wrap it around both roots. Then, tuck the roots into the magnolia petals and the bay leaves.

3. Put all items into the bag, then tie it with nine knots.

4. Carry the bag with you everywhere, and every week, drop a few drops of perfume into it.

Stay Mine Rum Candles

Want to make sure that your long-term lover stays in love with you and that they stay faithful as well? You have an easy option with these candle spells to ensure that your partner will stick around. With the right tools and ingredients, you can help make sure that your partner never leaves you behind. To complete this spell, you will need:

- A name paper

- Licorice root

- Orange peel

- Salt

- Rum

- White candles

Then, you will follow a few simple steps:

1. Write your name paper and your lover's name paper into your rum. Then, add in your licorice, orange, and salt.

2. Pray Psalm 139 over your bottle.

3. Shake the bottle nine times per day for nine days.

4. Write both your name and your lover's name onto a white candle's glass. Then, drop maybe three drops of rum onto the candle. Let it dry, and then light the candle.

5. Keep those candles lit and burning to keep your relationship happy and long-lasting. When one candle melts, simply anoint a new one with the rum and start again.

Get Him Hooked Hair Brush Spell

Want him to fall head over heels for you? You can! You just need to get started in the right way. First, you will need to have access to his hair so you can brush his hair. If you have got that, you can get moving with this particular spell. You will need a hairbrush and Love Me oil to complete this.

1. Brush and oil your own hair first.

2. Take the same brush that you used and brush his hair as well without taking out your hair. This will help to ensure that he keeps you o his mind.

Bake Him Pie Spell

Who doesn't love pie? If you want to give him one that will blow his mind, then start by baking one up just for him. However, if you want to make sure that your pie is especially addictive, you will want to add these steps to your recipe:

1. Add in cloves to help you rule over him.

2. Add in nutmeg to help win him over.

3. Add in a bit of your bathwater to make him addicted to you.

Wash His Sheets Spell

If you want to make sure that he'll be returning back to you every night, start by washing his sheets. While you do so, make sure that you recite the following:

1. Pray, "Love me [man's name] and come warm up my bed." Repeat this nine times over the washer. Then, add in a few squirts of your perfume to the washer as well.

2. Pray the same prayer nine more times over their bed when you make it as well.

New Love Vigil Spell

If you are ready to get new love in your life, you want to make sure that you do so effectively. You want to make sure that you have got that ability to love the people around you and to ensure that you are connecting that love where it needs to be. This love spell will help you to attract your own new relationships into your life before you know it. You will need:

- Olive Oil

- 7 Glass Red Candles

To complete this spell, you will go over the following:

1. Write out what you want from your lover. This should be complete—list out what you want and what you do not want. Then, roll it up and pray the list into the oil. Pray, "Please bring me a [person] who is [traits you need] and not [traits you want to avoid]."

2. Pray Psalm 61 into the oil.

3. Repeat steps 2 and 3, doing so over each of the candles. Add a few drops of oil to each one as well.

4. Burn your candles one at a time. Every day, once per day, pray Psalm 61 again over the candle. Then, start actively looking for a partner.

Burning Passion Candle Spell

Has your relationship been lacking that spark and passion that you have been missing? If so, why not bring it back? Why not do the Burning Passion Candle spell to get your beloved all worked up over you? Before you know it, he'll be going while for you and won't be able to keep his hands off of you. If you are ready to cause your partner to lust after you and bring that passion right back, all you have to do is this spell. You will need:

- One red 7-day candle

- Cinnamon

- Poppy seeds

- Ylang Ylang essential oil (you can also substitute in vanilla extract or jasmine essential oil if you cannot find this).

Then, you will follow a few simple steps to get your spell to work:

1. Poke three holes into the top of your candle.

2. Add in four drops of oil to one and a pinch of herbs to all other holes.

3. Recite the name of your lover twelve times over the candle.

4. If you are attempting to direct your spell toward a current lover, light the candle a couple of hours before your date is set

to happen. If, for a lover who is not present, such as an ex, you should instead burn their name paper a little over the candle over the next week. They should start going crazy for you.

Love Domination Jam Spell

Is your lover a bit much for you to handle? Do you need ways that you can do better to control the person that you love? Love domination spells are not for everyone… And you will want to be careful as well—while this can help you to gain the upper hand in your relationship, it can also go awry if you are not careful. Only perform this spell if you really want to control the person that you are interacting with. To complete this spell, you will need:

- ½ tsp cloves

- 2 cups chopped apple

- ½ cup cranberries

- 1 cup food-grade rose petals

- One small slow cooker

Then, you will follow these simple steps:

1. Mix all of your ingredients together into your slow cooker. Then, combine well with 1 cup of water.

2. Pray over your mixture with the following chant: "God gives me power over [lover's name]. Bind [lover's name] to my will." Do this nine times.

3. Cook on low for up to eight hours, adding more water if necessary.

4. Enjoy this together with your lover over brown bread and wait for the magic to kick in. Before you know it, your lover will be listening to you in no time.

No-Divorce

Ring Binding Spell

Are you worried that your partner may be about to divorce or break up with you? You might be worried that they've been talking about leaving you for someone else, or you have some other reason to be concerned. Either way, you should consider this No-Divorce Ring Binding Spell to help keep your spouse faithful and engaged in the relationship that you have.

This spell is simple; all you will need are:

- Your wedding rings

- Red thread

- Love oil

Then, you will follow these simple steps:

1. Take your red thread and anoint it with any love oil you prefer.

No-Divorce

2. Take the thread and use it to tie together your wedding ring to your partner's.

3. Hang the rings over the front door, and your husband or wife will always come back to your home to be with you.

Nature Tying Spell

Another spell to consider is tying the nature spell. This one is a bit more focused on the union between you and your spouse or partner. To complete this spell, you will need a few things that might be a bit harder to get your hands on than you might think if you do not have their willing participation. You will need:

- Two cotton threads

- Sexual fluids from both parties (or menstrual blood from the woman)

To complete this spell, you will need to follow these steps:

No-Divorce

1. Gather up your two threads. Then, use the sexual fluids to cover the threads, putting the fluids from him on one and the fluids from her on another.

2. Then, take the two threads and tie them into nine knots. Tie the knotted threads around the bedpost to make sure that your partner remains faithful and driven to be home with you.

Ward the Home Spell

If you are worried that other people may be interfering with your relationship, then you are in the right spot—you will be able to create a spell to help you keep others out of your business for good. To complete this spell, you will need to gather up the following:

- Your sexual fluids

- Salt

- Cloves

No-Divorce

Then, when you have everything, you must combine your salt, cloves, and fluids together. Then, sprinkle the mixture at the doorways into and out of your house. By doing so, you create a barrier between your home and your relationship with people who may conspire to damage it. This creation will help you to keep your partner closer than ever and prevent others from damaging your marriage.

Commitment Spell

If you are worried that your partner may not be committed to you entirely and you are afraid that it will damage your relationship, then you are in the right spot. By following through with the commitment spell you are about to learn, you will be able to keep your partner committed, one plate at a time. To complete this, you will need:

- Anise

- Cilantro

- Cumin

No-Divorce

- Fennel

- Rosemary

- Under

Then, you simply cook using these ingredients in your meal. After you have, pray Psalm 45 over the food and then serve it to your partner.

CHAPTER 7: SIMPLE SPELLS FOR LUCK

Who doesn't need a bit of luck every now and then? You want to ensure that you have got the right kind of luck that will help you to figure out what you are doing and when you are doing it. When you get through the luck in your relationships, you should start to see that you have got this power. You should start to see that you do have the ability to get through everything that you are doing at any point in time.

That boost of luck could be what you need to ensure that you get the job that you wanted. It could help you to get that new opportunity that you needed. It could grant you the ability to be the person that you want to be and to get the life that you want. Good luck is incredibly important, but if you do not have it, you are going to struggle. You need to figure out a way that you will be able to get through the world to improve your luck on your own. You will need to be able to take that control back for yourself, and thankfully, you have that opportunity. You just have to know what you are doing and how you are doing it.

Creating luck is relatively simple if you go back to the basics. Choosing out the right candles and the right herbs is important, but if you have the right tools, you can make sure that any bad luck that you have is reversed, and you can ensure that you are moving into the days of better luck. You just have to be in the right place at the right time.

When you can do that, you will find the success you are looking for.

As you read through this chapter, you will get all sorts of different spells. We'll look at spells that reverse bad luck. We'll see spells that bring good luck to you and more. When you start getting that better luck in your life, you will start to get that confidence that you are really looking for, and that will help you immensely. All you have to do is know what you are doing, and when you are doing it. Before you know it, you will be on track to ensuring that you have got the control and the influence you want.

Luck Reversal Spell

Is bad luck bringing you down? If so, it's time to start looking at what you can do to better it. Thankfully, you can choose-out ways to help to end that bad luck streak, and it all works with salt.

This spell has several different variations as well—you might see some places encourage you to change up the order of what you are doing. Others will encourage you to pray differently, or to add new prayers, or will use different fruits. This spell, however, is really simple to add to your life. You will simply need to do the following:

1. Carve your name three times into the skin of your orange.

2. Then, cut a hole onto the top and squeeze out most of the juice. Fill up the orange with salt.

3. Put your orange in the biggest window in your home. Then, let it sit there for nine days.

4. After the nine days are up, toss it out or bury it. You should see that your bad luck starts to reverse instead!

Lucky Cologne Spell

This spell is quite simple. You would be creating a cologne that you can use to spray on candles and mojos or even onto yourself if you wanted to. You can use it in baths as well if you want to start getting more luck in all aspects of your life. This spell will only require you to have three simple ingredients. You will need:

- Orange peel

- Rum

- Nutmeg

When you have gathered up all of your ingredients, you are ready to get started! It won't take you much to do so at all. You will simply follow these steps:

1. Take your orange and your nutmeg and toss them into a full bottle of rum.

2. Close the bottle and shake it while chanting, "All my kin, below and above, make me lucky, and make me love."

3. Then, put your bottle into a sunny spot and leave it there for nine days. Every day, shake it and repeat your chant.

4. Use the oil on candles (making sure they're unlit first), mojos, baths, or anywhere else that you want to help bring luck and joy to your life.

Prosper Me Pumpkin Spell

If you want to get some more luck into your home, you want to bring in some of the luckiest things that you can. In this spell, you will be working with a pumpkin, pecans, ginger, brown sugar, and rum to create a spell that will not only smell amazing as you work through it but will start bringing good luck, prosperity, and love into your home. Are you ready? This spell is quite simple. You will just do the following:

1. Start by cutting open your pumpkin carefully. You are leaving the seeds inside of it.

2. Then, carve the names of the people you want to be blessed with good luck into the sides of the pumpkin, right into the skin.

3. Put all ingredients inside of the pumpkin and toss in any personal belongings or effects of those who you want to have blessed.

4. Then, if possible, dig a fire pit into burning the pumpkin. You will bury the pumpkin in the soil, then have a fire on top of it while you let the fire burn. Share a meal while you want the fire to burn out.

5. If you can't dig a fire pit, then you can bake the pumpkin in your oven set to 200 all day long.

6. Bury the pumpkin either in your yard or in the nearest crossroads to get the effect intended.

Prosper Me Wash

Does your home business need a bit of extra luck to ensure that it stays afloat I these trying times? Do you want your home to be protected and lucky? If so, then you might want to consider the "Prosper Me" wash that you can use to bring prosperity to the spaces where it is used to clean. This creates a floor wash that you can use to open up possibilities, welcoming the prosperity that you are looking for. To complete this, you will need lemongrass, magnolia petals, and peppermint.

1. Take two large handfuls of each of your herbs and toss them into 2 quarts of water.

2. Then, while you boil the water, pray Psalm 23 over your pot.

3. Then, take out your herbs and bury them.

4. Wash your floors, walls, door frames, and other surfaces of the home or business that you are trying to bless.

5. Do this five times over five weeks, choosing Fridays as the day of choice.

CHAPTER 8: SIMPLE SPELLS FOR MONEY

If what you are looking for in your life is money, you are in the right place. Now, there's nothing wrong with being motivated to bring money into your life. After all, we all need it along the way. We all need to find ways that we can pay for our expenses, and sometimes, money can be a bit tight.

If you are in need of spells that will help you to get the money where you need it, then you are in the right spot. With the spells that you will be provided here, you can create the openings in your life so you can bring that money into your life as well. Before you know it, you will have the information that you will need to help you to get those added effects that you are looking for. Before you know it, you will be in that position of having the added benefit of getting the wealth you need.

From bathing to anointing to otherwise attracting the money that you need, you can get this information and make use of it to benefit yourself. When you do this, you will make it clear that you have the power to be the powerful one that you want to be. All you need to do is get started, and this chapter is here to help you.

Golden Prosper Bath Spell

So, you want to attract wealth. Thankfully, with this simple bath, you can do just that. This bath will use several herbs and plants that will help you to attract wealth and money right into your life. All you will have to do is know what you are doing to make it drawn to you. You will need a few plants in particular for this: Sassafras leaves, goldenseal root, and marigold petals will come together to help you to trigger that influx of money where you need it. If you want to complete this spell, you will do the following:

2. Start by taking two handfuls of sassafras leaves with one of goldenseal root and two handfuls of marigold petals.

3. Mix all of your herbs with one gallon of holy water. Then, boil it.

4. After the water reaches a rolling boil, turn off the heat and allow it to cool. When you can safely handle the water, strain out the herbs, and bury them to dispose of them properly.

5. Then, recite Psalm 4 over the mixture.

6. As you recite your Psalm, stir the water clockwise.

7. To bless a person, add this mixture into their bathwater. Then, when the person is done bathing, they should then allow themselves to air dry.

8. If you want to bless a home, you can use this added to the floor water or cleaning water that you are using.

9. If you want to bless a business, use it in a spray bottle and spritz it everywhere, especially onto fabrics. Allow it to air dry.

Protect My Money Spell

If you already have money, or if you are afraid that you will lose your money soon, you can use this spell to help yourself to protect the money that you have. You can use this spell to help to hold onto what you do have so you can ensure that you do not lose anything. Protecting yourself from that loss means that you can ensure that you feel more confident in the money that you do have. To complete this spell, you will need five finger grass, devil's claw pods, goldenseal root, a green cloth, and your name paper. Then, you will follow these simple steps:

1. Start by praying over each herb. You should recite: "Protect my money, bring my money to me, keep my money with me."

2. Then, dress the name paper with any oils that you want to use.

3. Fold up the herbs inside of your name paper. Then, tie the name paper and your herbs into the green cloth and hide the sachet somewhere safe in your home so you can protect it.

Quick Cash Fire Spell

To get that money to come into your home quickly or to get it in a business, sometimes, you need the Quick Cash Fire spell. This spell is simple and only requires three key ingredients to get started with it. With just bay leaves, cinnamon, and nutmeg, you can get that cash flowing. This spell will require you to follow these simple steps:

1. Start by taking all ingredients and pray over them all. Your prayer should be sincere and should specify the amount of money that you will need. This is perfect when kept as short and sweet as possible.

2. Then, take your herbs and burn them all over an open fire or charcoal.

3. Wave the smoke and pull it over your body, focusing on your hands and face.

4. Then, wait. You should have the money to arrive soon.

Emergency Money Pineapple Spell

This spell will help you to get that money that you need into your business or home when it is urgently needed. It is something that you can do with just a few simple tools and ingredients, and if you gather them up and follow-through, you should see the money that you need within a few days of casting the spell. This is perfect for you if you really need it and should help you to get exactly what you needed. To complete this spell, you will need to first gather your supplies. You need some green thread, pineapple, wine, and a petition that dictates how much money you need. To follow through with this spell, then, you will follow these steps:

1. Start by cutting off the top of your pineapple. Without damaging the outside, remove the inside fruit from the

pineapple. Then, put in your petition that dictates how much money you need.

2. Pour in the wine into your pineapple until you have mostly filled up the cavity.

3. Then, pray over the pineapple, reciting Psalm 23 three times.

4. Place the top of the pineapple back onto it and then secure it, tying it with a green thread. Then, leave it at a crossroads and wait. You should see the money in a few days.

Green Money Bag Spell

This spell is incredibly simple to put together if you know what you are doing. And, putting it together can help you to bring that money that you really need in your life sooner. Do you need a higher income? Do you need some good luck with the money? Then you are in the right spot—you want to use this to help achieve it.

This spell will, however, need a bit more than most of the others have. You will need:

- Your name paper

- Pine needles

- A green bag

- Three pennies (They have to be shiny!)

- Iron pyrite

Then, when you have everything that you will need for this spell, you will get started. Follow these simple steps to get going:

1. Begin by setting up your name paper. Add on any moneydrawing oil if you want to include it, but this is not strictly necessary.

2. Then, crush the needles up. Then, rub your coins and pyrite into the needles.

3. Fold your needles, coins, and pyrite right into your naming paper and carefully tuck it into your bag. Tie the bag up.

4. Keep this bag in your pockets at all times for that extra bit of luck and to boost your income. You should have some income-related opportunities appearing shortly!

If you do not have any pennies for this, you can use any traditional coin to do so. Just make sure that any coins that you do choose are low value, and they must be shiny.

Financial Relief Candle Spell

This spell is perfect to attract a bit of wealth into your life immediately if you are in need. When you need to get that cash in your pocket, you can use this spell. With a few simple tools, you can bring in some amount of cash, with the value being no higher than $5,000. However, remember this—the spell will only work if you really do need the money for something that is essential to you. If you want the money for something extra that is not necessary, then this spill will not work. Make sure that you are only asking for what you need and nothing more. For this spell, you will need:

- Green 7-Day candle

- Black tea

- Peppermint essential oil

- Ginger

Then, you will follow a few simple steps:

1. Poke three holes into the top of the candle.

2. Drop four drops of oil into one hole, then add a bit of herb into the other two.

3. Write down the number representing the amount of money that you need. Remember, it should be only what you need. Then, sign your name three times over.

4. Then, pray, "Holy ones, help me. Bring me a gift and supply

what I need." Recite this twelve times over your candle.

5. Then, you will light the candle every day, praying over it each day upon lighting it. Wait, and if the spirits think you need the money, they will provide it.

CHAPTER 9: SIMPLE SPELLS FOR PROTECTION

We all need some protection sometimes, especially when we are dabbling in magic that involves spirits. When you have decided to enter a graveyard for magic, or if you find that you are starting to have some worse luck or outcomes than you normally would, you might find yourself wondering if you picked up some negativity, a hex, or even a curse somewhere along the way. The thought makes sense, too—if you are getting involved with this kind of magic, you have to be prepared for the fact that not all spirits are good or benign. You have to acknowledge that sometimes, you will need to protect yourself.

The spells in this chapter are aimed toward protection, with it being preemptive. This means that we are looking at spells that are primarily going to try to stop anything negative from happening in the first place. After all, prevention is usually the best treatment. Are you ready to ensure that you are not getting taken advantage of? Are you ready to ensure that at the end of the day, you are kept safe from harm? Are you ready to prevent yourself from being hurt? Let's get started!

Protection from Harm Bottle Spell

This first spell is meant to help you to keep away harm, injustice, and abuse. If you are afraid that you will be unfairly targeted for any reason, you will want to have this spell on your side. You will want to begin by gathering up everything that you will need. For this spell, you will require the following:

- Name paper, connecting it to your target

- Black feathers, to obscure your location from harm

- Oregano, to keep the law away

- Hard liquor, to give strength and courage

- Salt, to protect you from danger

Then, when you have all of your ingredients, you can begin. You will go over these steps to keep yourself safe:

2. Begin by writing the name papers of everyone that you are targeting. These are the people you want to keep safe, such as yourself, friends, family, and other loved ones. When you have your list of people that you wish to protect,t you can put the names into the bottle of liquor.

3. Then, add all other ingredients one at a time. As you add them, pray Psalm 91 over each one.

4. Then, seal the bottle up with whatever you have on hand.

5. Shake up the bottle 11 times. Then, leave it outside your back door whenever someone that you have listed on the name paper that is in the bottle is in danger.

6. When not in use, store it in a safe place.

Reputation Saver Spell

Is your reputation under attack by someone? Have the gossips in your town taken things a bit too far? If so, you are not alone by any means. This gossips can sometimes ruin reputations, and that can ruin lives. However, you can also fend off that gossip and protect your reputation if you know what you are doing. By making use of this spell, you can ensure that at the end of the day, you are protected from harm and able to get through the situation relatively unscathed.

To complete this spell, you will need a few key ingredients:

- Sunflower seeds

- Dirt from a crossroads

- Reversing oils

- Silver dime

- Your name paper

Take the supplies for this spell and get ready. To complete this spell, you will need to do the following:

1. Take a piece of paper with torn edges and write out your name paper.

2. Put nine drops of your chosen intention oil onto the paper.

3. Fold all of the other ingredients inside of the paper, securing it with a string if you want to.

4. Then, pray over your bag, saying, "I bind all who speak ill of me," and repeat this nine times over the bag.

5. Carry the bag in any situation where you worry that others may attempt to harm your reputation. It should help to shield you from harm around the way, and that will keep you nice and safe.

Storm Haven Spell

This spell is designed to protect someone when they are busy traveling in situations where they are in danger from a storm. This particular spell can be great if you know that people are in the path of a hurricane or tornado or if you are simply worried that some sort of natural disaster is going to strike. This is an old, strong spell that is meant to protect individuals as much as possible. If you want to use this spell, you will simply follow a few simple steps to ensure that they are safe. But, first, you will need comfrey root, a name paper for the person you are attempting to protect, and white cotton thread. With that gathered, you can begin the spell.

1. Start by dressing the name paper with any protection oils that you want to use. Then, take the comfrey root and wrap it up inside of the paper. Pray Psalm 22 over the root while wrapping it up completely with white thread: Then, leaving some string loose, tie it off.

2. Tie the spell over the door of your home to protect the house and those in it. You can also wear it around the neck like an amulet to protect yourself personally as well.

Power and Protect Hand Spell

If you need to protect yourself from love magic, black magic, or harm, this is the spell for you. By using this spell, you can ensure that you are shielded from any magic that might cause problems for you later on. If you want to do so, you will need a few ingredients that will help you to put everything together. You will need the following:

- High John Root

- Urine from your target (or cologne if you can't get urine)

- Red thread

- Name paper

- Salt

Then, you will go over the following steps to ensure that you get the protection that you are looking for:

1. Start by writing the target's name paper. If you are the one being protected, then you are the intended target. Then, after you have the name paper, soak it with urine or cologne.

2. Cover the paper with a sprinkle of salt. Then, recite Psalm 91 over it.

3. Wrap the paper around the High John Root.

4. Then, bind the paper with the red thread, wrapping it around the root.

5. Allow the root to dry in the sun for three days. Then, carry it with you after that. Every Monday, feed it with Florida water, cologne, or more urine.

Protection from

Evil Candle Spell

If you are concerned about spiritual or other harm, this is a spell that you can cast to protect yourself. The purpose of this spell is to prevent harm from coming to you, or to other people, or even other objects if you were to write down the right things. When you use this spell, you are able to protect yourself and ensure that at the end of the day, you are not taken advantage of by evil.

This spell only needs a few simple tools:

- A blue 7-day candle

- Dried onion

- Cloves

- Camphor oil

Then, you will follow these simple steps to create the intended effect:

1. Start by poking three holes in the top of your candle.

2. In one hole, drip in four drops of your camphor oil.

3. In the other two holes, ad a bit of each herb.

Protection from

4. Write the name of the person, place, or thing that you want to protect onto paper and place it under the candle.

5. Pray Psalm 91 over your candle. Light it and burn it daily, reciting the Psalm every time you light it.

Nightmares Spell

Whether you, a loved one or a child is suffering from nightmares, you may find that you are losing out on a lot of sleep that you could otherwise be getting. To fix this problem, however, you have a simple option: You can follow a protection spell to help yourself to cleanse out the evil spirits that are causing the nightmares in the first place. Completing this spell is incredibly simple, too—all you need is salt and yourself! With that, you can ensure that the room is cleansed of evil energy and spirits. To complete this spell, you will do the following:

1. Sprinkle the floor, the furniture, the doorways, and the mattress in the room with salt.

2. Pray Psalm 91 over the room.

3. Then, sweep up the salt and take it out of the room. This will help to cleanse out the room, and you should find yourself enjoying peaceful sleep as a result!

Protection from

Illness Spell

If you are worried about yourself or someone else getting sick, you can follow this very simple protection spell to prevent it and help you to assuage your concerns. Completing this spell will be very simple— to do so, you will simply need the following:

- A hag stone (a stone that naturally already has a hole in it)

- Red string or thread

- Florida water

Then, when you have everything that you will need, you will simply follow these steps:

1. Take the stone and hang it on your red string.

2. Tie the string over the bed of the person you intend to protect.

3. Every week, wash the stone with Florida water to clean the evil before it can cause illness. You have to wash away the evil with the Florida water to protect the individual.

Protection from

Losing Children Spell

Are you worried about losing your child in some way? Maybe you fear that they will be kidnapped. Maybe you have concerns that they may wander off and get lost. Or, maybe you are worried you might even forget them somewhere! No matter the reason for your concern, any parent wants to know that their child is going to be safe, so you will need this spell to help you to achieve just that. This spell is incredibly simple to perform, and you will be able to keep your kid protected and at home. You will need:

- Dirt from your front yard

- Dirt from a churchyard (or from a crossroads)

- Your child's shoes

Then, when you have everything, you will put a bit of the dirt from your yard into your child's *left* shoe. You will take a bit of the dirt from the churchyard and sprinkle it into your child's *right* foot. After doing this, they should have the protection to keep them at home with you, safe and sound.

Protection from

Bullies for Children Spell

If you are concerned that your child may be bullied at school or somewhere else, you may want to perform a spell to protect them, especially if they have complaints about being bullied from the past. For this spell, you will be able to give them a little bit of extra protection, and it will only take you a few minutes. You will need:

- A hard stone

- Holy water

When you have the necessary tools, you will do the following:

1. Take the stone and bless it with your holy water.

2. Then, you will tell the stone, "You are [name of the child you are protecting]. You give him/her strength and protect him/her from all harm." Repeat this nine times.

3. Then, put the stone somewhere warm in your kitchen and keep it there for the fullest effect. Your child should report that the bullying has come to a halt!

CHAPTER 10: SIMPLE SPELLS FOR JUSTICE

No one wants to intentionally be wronged. However, when it does happen, you can find yourself needing to take action. You can find yourself in a position where you have to make some sort of change to ensure that at the end of the day, you can protect yourself or to get your own justice. That is where this chapter and the spells that you will find here come into play. By being able to defensively protect yourself from harm, you can ensure that you are kept safe. You can ensure that you are free from legal or physical harm because you will ensure that you do not get any undue harm your way. From being able to cast out things that are harmful to be able to bring things to even ground, you will find that this chapter is going to be quite useful to you.

Be Gone Banishing Fire Spell

Is something in your life a nuisance that you need gone sooner rather than later? Is there something causing you problems? If so, you might need to banish it. Whether you are banishing people who are no good to you or trying to get rid of something, this fire can help you to get that justice for yourself. You will need:

- Bay leaves

- White onion skin

- Peanut shells

- Lemongrass

When you put together this spell, you will do the following:

1. Build a small fire in a safe location, preferably outside, so you can burn safely.

2. Then, on each bay leaf, write something that you wish to banish from your life. This is where you would write down the names of people who have wronged or harmed you.

3. Mix all ingredients together into a bowl, stirring the whole thing counter-clockwise. Then, pray over your mixture, "That which I have written, send away forever." Repeat this nine times.

4. Burn all herbs. Be mindful of the smoke—you should not be inhaling it.

5. Wait for the entire fire to burn out. Then, allow it to cool and bury the ashes. Within the next few months, those things should be banished.

Baby Daddy Spell

Does your child's father claim that he is not actually related to the child? If so, you are not alone. A lot of fathers simply are not ready or willing to believe that their children are actually theirs. This is unfair for the children and unfair for the fathers and the mothers. However, you can use this spell to encourage the father of your child to acknowledge the truth. Keep in mind that this will only work if the child is truly his own. To complete this spell, you will need the following:

- Truth oil

- Tobacco leaves

- Dirt dauber nest

- Child's hair

- The name paper of the father

To complete this spell, you will do the following:

1. Start by dressing the name paper with three dots of truth oil. Then, fold the items into the paper. Pray over it, "[Father's name]; this is your [son/daughter]. Come and lift them up!" Repeat this nine times.

2. Carry the packet with you and repeat your nine iterations of the prayer nine times per day for nine days.

3. If the father acknowledges the truth within the nine days, save the packet somewhere safe.

4. If he does not acknowledge the truth, bury the packet in the churchyard with a coin. This will curse his money until he supports his child.

Quick Reconciliation Spell

Are you in a bit of a tough spot with someone right now but wish you weren't? You are not alone—you can use this spell to help to heal the quarrel before it can be allowed to fester any longer. This particular spell will require you to first write out all of Psalm 32, take a pink candle, eight pins, and honey. When you have everything, you can start the spell.

1. Begin by writing out all of Psalm 32.

2. After writing everything out, write on the back of the paper, the name of the person with who you wish to reconcile, and do so three times.

3. Then, carve the name of the person you wish to reconcile with into the candle three times.

4. Place the pins around the candle on the bottom of the plate in a circle. Then, cover the pins with honey (this encourages the pain of the argument to be forgotten).

5. Burn over the next three days. Every day, repeat Psalm 32.

Psychic Peace Spell

Do you need peace of mind? Do you need to block out some messages or communication that is harmful to you? If so, you might need this spell to help you. This spell is actually a drink that you will consume. To create it, you will need:

- One orange peel

- ¼ cup honey

- 3 cups of pomegranate juice

- Three lemongrass stalks

Then, you will follow these steps to ensure that you have got the right protection:

1. Start by boiling the juice, honey, orange, and lemongrass until the liquid starts to thicken a bit.

2. Pray Psalm 10 over the mixture while you stir counterclockwise.

3. Pray Psalm 4 over the mixture, stirring clockwise.

4. Drink before bed each day for the next nine days. You should be able to prevent any sort of unwanted spiritual connection.

CONCLUSION

And that brings us to the end of this book! You have now been guided through the key tenets to beginning with Hoodoo, and you have been given several key spells that you can start to use yourself if you want to start practicing on your own. If you want to be the person that you can be and if you want to be able to figure out how to tap into your connections with your ancestral spirits, then you have gotten the starting point.

Hopefully, you feel a bit closer to the spirits and your own potential powers as well. This is not easy, and as a beginner, you may find that you struggle at times, but remember this: You were BORN to do this. You were born with the skills. You were born with the ability. You were born with the power to be the one using these skills to be the best version of you that you could become. All you have to do is make sure that you are in the right mindset and work to learn.

Thank you for choosing this book as your introduction to Hoodoo, and hopefully, you are ready to get started, or at the very least, you are convinced to keep looking into the art! You can do this if you keep putting in the effort. You can make this work for you. You just have to be willing to try. And, if you can do that, then you can do anything. So, what are you waiting for? It's time to start!

And finally, if you found that the information in this book was useful to you or that it helped you to get started, please consider leaving a review on Amazon with your experience! It would be greatly appreciated to hear what you think and feel about the content so the next book can be even better!

CPSIA information can be obtained
at www.ICGtesting.com
Printed in the USA
LVHW052014250121
677443LV00017B/3054